Watch Your Head

poems by Kevin Rabas

Press   Emporia, KS

Also by Kevin Rabas

Bird's Horn
Lisa's Flying Electric Piano
Spider Face
Sonny Kenner's Red Guitar
Green Bike (with Simmons & Graves)
Eliot's Violin
Songs for My Father
All That Jazz
Late for Cymbal Line
Like Buddha-Calm Bird
Everyone Just Wants to Drum

Watch Your Head
Copyright © 2019 Kevin Rabas

All rights reserved. No part of this publication may be reproduced, distributed, or transmitted in any form or by any means, without prior written permission of the publisher.

This is a work of fiction. The names, characters, places, and incidents are either a product of the author's imagination or used fictitiously, and any resemblance to actual persons living or dead, business establishments, events, or locals is entirely coincidental.

To contact Kevin Rabas, send to:

Kevin Rabas
PO Box 274
Emporia, KS 66801
or
krabas3@yahoo.com
or
www.kevinrabas.com

Published by Kellogg Press
1114 Commercial St.
Emporia, Kansas 66801
kelloggpress.com

Printed in the United States of America

Curtis Becker, Editor/Layout and Design
curtis@curtisbeckerbooks.com

Eric Sonnakolb, Cover Design

Dave Leiker, Photography

ISBN: 978-0-578-52760-4

Praise for Watch Your Head

In his latest collection of poetry we see Kevin Rabas share snapshots from his past and ultimately, his humanity. In "Watch Your Head" Kevin gives his voice to relationships, loss, vulnerability, change, uncertainty, and healing. There is also that familiar theme found throughout his body of work as well, music. With well crafted words, Kevin puts flesh and blood on the page, letting us feel his art and, in the end, catch a glimpse into a life not entirely different than our own. This is a collection worthy of reflection and praise.

–Kerry Moyer, *Dirt Road*

Take a twenty-year step back—a transformative time for Kevin Rabas. Between a head injury, divorce, friends parting ways, and meeting the love of his life, these poems bring the reader through some of the deepest introspection and observation we have seen from Rabas yet. Some of these poems emanate a warm light and tickle of romance, bravery and confidence–the curiosities of young adulthood. Other poems are reminders that even when all seems lost, we can use our poetic voice to find the way home.

–Linzi Garcia, *Thank You*

for Lisa

Table of Contents

Sauce	3
Our Divorce	4
[Grandfather]	5
Adrie, the Prodigy	6
My Arms Open	8
Speedy	9
For Dennis W–	10
Knocking Out Walls with Chet Baker	12
Artt's Sabbatical	13
Together Now	14
Our Home	15
Saxophone	16
Pheasant	17
[Typing]	18
[Light you]	19
After the Fire	20
Jumper	21
[Swim]	22

[Poker Party]	23
Annabelle	24
Winter Nap	25
[For James]	26
[Behind the Candle's Flame]	27
Hole in the Wall	28
My Father's Words	29
[Lost Days]	30
Live by the Light	31
Yard Lines	32
Last Road Trip (alt.)	33
Answers	34
Phoenix	35
Sunset	36
Accidents	37
Holding on So Long	38
Artt Frank's Jab	39

I never knew what you meant	40
[New Orleans, That Road Trip]	41
Behind These Doors	42
Apartment Warming	43
Grazie	44
Make an End to Mourning	45
Anna Karenina	46
Spring in the City	47
Spring and Fall	48
Swim Team Tryouts	49
I have known...	50
[Our Time]	52
[Pomegranate]	53
Chet's Unlikely Second Rise	54
Waiting	56
[for Doug Talley, on sax]	57
Jazz Body Language	58

[Radio Voice]	59
[Merry Christmas, Kevin]	60
Voice	61
[Moving in]	62
Fall Golf	63
[We took this town]	64
Lend Me Your Lips	65
Buried out Back	66
Because I Stayed	68
Fool Self	69
Menninger's	70
Dreams	71
Not My Last Love Poem	72

Introduction

I wrote to help me through a hard time in 1999. Head injured, going through a divorce, jobless, I wrote these poems to help heal myself and make sense of things. (It all started when I got knocked down in a pick up basketball game.) Some of the poems in this book are love and loss poems for my ex-wife. Some are poems for my new love, Lisa. Others are about my time in Arkansas* (1995), where I attended university briefly, studying creative writing and jazz. So, this collection roughly covers 1995-2000. Much of what I wrote during that time, I kept, but no one needs to read. The gems Linzi Garcia** selected and ordered. I then polished these selected poems slightly, aiming to preserve most of what was there, as is. For instance, I had a different concept of the line break in 1999, leaning more heavily towards a short pause at the end of the line; or I used enjambment that comes in chunks with each line constituting a unit, such as a prepositional phrase. I tried for the most part to preserve that approach. In terms of content, I didn't add much, just took out some of the understood, the excess. I was higher on passion, back then, and lower on craft—or had a freer sense of craft, a style that was more fluid, confessional, Beat: enamored more with direct statement than I am now. This collection is a little like a trash bin set on fire: wild, but contained. Enjoy its fiery light.

—Kevin Rabas, Friday 31 May 2019, 8:22 pm, Subway sandwich shop in Walmart, Emporia, Kansas

* University of Arkansas - Fayetteville
** Linzi Garcia is one of my students and helps me as a Graduate Assistant at Emporia State.

Watch Your Head

Sauce

All day you kept the pot simmering.
The sauce is the most important part,
you say, and like love it takes a while
to make its own taste, make its mark
on the heart and kidneys, and starts
with the prick of the taste buds,
sinking in between the bumps, the fleshy
    mountains
which guide our insides, connect us to our
nose and throats, our pasta innards,
tangled and heaped.

You let me add only the mushrooms.
You crush the oregano between your petite fingers,
crackling each flake like an autumn leaf.
I know I could stand here beside you
and this hot pot for days.

for my ex-wife

Kevin Rabas

Our Divorce

I miss you this evening, my love,
although I have lost you.
You shaped the plates
with your own hands
the plates we used to eat—
from clay the cups,
the saucers, the pitcher
with its flamboyant handle,
like something playful
to hold: a banana bike grip,
a hula hoop.

Tonight, someone else takes hold
of our HUD house banister,
someone else walks the kitchen
somewhat in hunger.

Although my in-laws
took all the plates, I have
one cup. I keep
my pens in it.

Watch Your Head

[Grandfather]

I put my grandfather's ring on
this afternoon, a shiny
gold band.

I am learning golf, alone.
I swing with a great arc
and end like I'm carrying a torch.
The upstroke must clinch it.
Don't bother to follow the ball
with your eyes, your head.
It will fall. It will.

While retrieving the balls
I clown a bit, use the club
like a a regal cane
when I step, swing
full circle, going
to town like a man in a tux
on a Gates Bar-B-Q sign.

My grandfather might move like this.
He is from that hero sect,
flew planes, taught aeronautics
to new pilots in WWII.
Even when he looked down
he saw sky.

Kevin Rabas

Adrie, the Prodigy

Those evenings in your apartment
in Fayetteville, Arkansas
you balanced your violin
against your neck
as if the instrument
had always been
a limb, part of you.

You played classical jigs
that made us
want to dance.

You knew
Bartok's passion,
staccato accents,
fat as knuckles rapped
against an oak table top,
sharp as metal plates
attached to the bottoms
of dancing shoes.

You were the school prodigy.
At seventeen, even the department
heads looked up to you.
They knew you had the skill
and passion to pass them,
and so they made way, handing
you the most difficult tunes.

Your long dark hair fell in waves
along your delicate back. You would brush
strands behind your ear before you played.
Dressing before recitals, you would ask me

Watch Your Head

if you looked too auspicious. Never,
I would always say. Never. Go on and shine.

Kevin Rabas

My Arms Open
for Lisa, ala Neruda

My arms open,
a harbor, where
the nets
can hold water,
where the fork
can hold soup
like the spoon.

You hold the smell
of night on you,
secret scents
of distant stars, fires
which no incense can match,
a light oil around your body,
dark pond water, steeped
between autumn leaves.

I hold my heat
for you in my heart,
which would glow
orange as an ember
if you called.

When I hold you,
ask me what I desire,
and I will say
only what I can hold.

Watch Your Head

Speedy

When the exterminators came
knocking on the door
of your apartment,
you pulled the sheet over your head,
told them there ain't no bugs here,
but they sprayed anyway.

They named you "Speedy"
for your fast tap dance.
These days, though, you move
as the turtle does,
one foot from the shell,
then the other, shuffle
along the sidewalk
as old men do.

During your last set,
you sing "Don't Get Around
Much Anymore" twice,
because you have forgotten
you already played that one.

Kevin Rabas

For Dennis W–

You left this town
with your horn
and one dream:
to make it in Chicago.

Already in Kansas City
you had paid dues,
playing for peanuts and beer,
hitting the jams:
arriving with your head in the air,
your horn uplifted,
departing beaten,
almost dragging your saxophone
across the floor
inside its hard black plastic case,
a bed, a coffin, a suitcase,
but a way of life ticked inside.
And you would rise again
late in the night
next week, returning
to the cutting ground, a stage
with hot lights and swift changes,
always so many changes taking place.

You would change your clothes
to fit the styles you were trying on:
Lester Young, Buster Douglas, Pharoah Sanders,
John Coltrane, Stan Getz, Eddie Harris, more.
You wore a purple suit one night,
a lima bean green one the next.
You grew a mustache
and donned a brown city Kangol cap.
To the ladies you called yourself

Watch Your Head

a stallion, and you
galloped your way
across the chords.

Kevin Rabas

Knocking Out Walls with Chet Baker

for Artt Frank

Days, we knocked out walls
that summer. Nights,
we played clubs.
You were good
with the hammer,
steady, sure.
You bent from the brick
and swung. I knew you
would break through,
would find your way
into a woman's heart.
You hefted your horn, held it
first like a hammer,
then like a child.
You knew just how
to swing one note
into another, how to
breathe into metal,
make it warm.

Watch Your Head

Artt's Sabbatical

Your bible is held together
by grey duct tape,
its pages highlighted
and margins filled with pencil
scratches. You studied
the good book
by flashlight, living in a car
back east. You learned
how to punch and how
to receive a blow—
a welterweight boxer,
a drummer, street preacher,
until a woman found you
and brought you
back to this jazzy world
of tortured melodies
and cold cold bridges
in between.

Kevin Rabas

Together Now

I have found the voice within me
that can call you back to me,
It is not easy singing this low,
pulling my chest in as if
from a punch.

It is not easy to cry,
to bray like a grown man,
to call like a wolf,
to howl like John the Baptist in the wild.

I have eaten my honey and locusts.
I have chopped enough wood
for the fire that will burn enough nights
to prove to you that I am strong now.

I am gentle enough now
to hold out my fingers
and call doves.

Bring with you what you will.
Know that none of that matters.
The earth calls out to us.
It is time to move together now.
Do not move away.

Watch Your Head

Our Home

We rest this afternoon
on your red flannel sheets,
while the city rushes below.
A lot of my life is left,
and I am glad—
for your company, ready
for our clothes to gather
together in a shared chest,
our socks and shirts
coupling, our keys and coins piling
on top, our bodies standing together
in your full-length mirror,
our shoes nestled
near the foot of our bed.
These will be the days
we call our own,
our flat, our horizon,
our home, this apartment.

Kevin Rabas

Saxophone

I am close enough
to hear the horn's
keys click
along the long-necked
saxophone. Soft shoe.
I know love,
and this is what
it sounds like—

evenings in the dark city,
a glass
close at hand.

Watch Your Head

Pheasant

I bring home
in my orange vest
our bird, our supper tonight.

I clean and cut him out back in the grass.
We invite company, and the man speaks
of his own father, how he once
taught him to fish and hunt.
I offer him a knife, but he declines.
He has known blood and dirt
and likes to keep himself well-soaped.

I hesitate
to show him
my own hands.

Kevin Rabas

[Typing]

Let your fingers rise from the keyboard in waves.
Clack down your thoughts and what you want.
Let me know where you are tonight.

Watch Your Head

[Light you]

I will wait for you
this evening
under my lamp post,
my trumpet
tipped to the sidewalk.
You know the pose.

Bring your party dress
and your feather boa.
String the Christmas lights
around your body,
and I will light you.

Kevin Rabas

After the Fire

I have waited here
in the wilderness,
watching the new trees
sprout and grow,
the ceratinous cones
released by the fire.
Everywhere dead, grey,
lodgepole pines
stand still as spooked ghosts.
I am here with a message
for you. Don't move.

Watch Your Head

Jumper

I have heard the call
from far off,
a man's shout
from a bridge;
just tell the tale
simply. I will listen.
Don't worry.
I won't
jump.

Kevin Rabas

[Swim]

Don't struggle. Swim.
Find rhythm
in the water. Breathe
from the edge
of your mouth.

Know that there will
always be more water
to move through.

Watch Your Head

[Poker Party]

The stakes are lower now,
late, and I play full out,
risking my quarters
to a bad hand
which could
be made good,
if only for the luck
of a straight.

And when we end,
I give all
of my quarters back,
except what
I came with.

Kevin Rabas

Annabelle

I have known your offer,
a bed on the floor.

I have eaten your supper,
which we cooked together, fearing
you added your mojo
to the sauce
when I wasn't looking.
You'll keep me this way.

I have seen photos
of your former boyfriend,
his chest bared.

I have watched you whittle
reeds for your oboe, red thread
kept within reach.
You tie pieces together,
then yell
through the window
to the street.

"I have made it," you say.
"The perfect reed!
Tune to this."

Watch Your Head

Winter Nap

Outside
a plane paints
a thin cirrus cloud,
which sinks
into the trees.

When will I
leave this house?

The pampas plumes
wave in winter wind.
I know it must be soon.

The chickadees
move in groups.
They turn and
scatter together,
lithe as planes
in formation.

Snow tops
the stone posts.
The mail arrives
at noon.

The doorbell rings,
and I am awakened.
Seven Christmas cards.

I know
I will not sleep so
soundly for the rest
of my life.

Kevin Rabas

[For James]

Last night
we slept
on your floor.

This morning
we ate your muffins
with black tea.

Your shower now
must have
smaller soap.

We left
few traces
of our stay—

and quarters
for your wash.

Watch Your Head

[Behind the Candle's Flame]

Where are you,
my love,
on this cold night?

On which dark windows
may I find
your reflection,
your breath, fogging
the glass?

I am behind
the candle's flame,
my pen
fast to the page.

Kevin Rabas

Hole in the Wall

You have made it through
the witching hour,
your fist caught
in the sheetrock wall.

Sometimes the nightmares
follow you. Sometimes
you take it too far.

Watch Your Head

My Father's Words

Tomorrow, I may lose my job.
Thirty years I've worked
for one construction company.
I know how
superintendents go.
They crack up.

You find them
in the bughouse.
They lose it. The plans
still in their minds, if not
in their hands. They know
the pour comes this Thursday
at three, concrete on its way.
There are footings
to pour, sidewalks
to consider. Rebar
that must already
be in place. Keep your hardhats
on tight, boys.
Your heads level.
Don't look up
unless you must
or you may catch it
in the eye.

Kevin Rabas

[Lost Days]

When the sun falls
behind these Flint Hills,
the sunflowers
bow. A seed spills
to soil. I remember
the lost days
of my life.

Watch Your Head

Live by the Light

There is no use hoping
that we will meet again.
I am certain now
we won't.

I have waited for you
at the top of the stair
for months now
when the sun goes.

I know that you
won't arrive.

We won't go on.
We'll fade.

And only
our memories
will haunt us
at night.

Some evenings
I hear your voice.
I see your face
in the face of another,
and I lie down
in tears
until the giants of night
pass me.

I sleep with the lamp on.
There is no reason
to wait
for the sun.

Kevin Rabas

Yard Lines

I've known the joy
of golden cymbals
clashing in the sun.
This afternoon
our time marked
in paces and yard lines.
Beside us march
the tubas, and behind us
trombones.
In front we feel
the swish of a red skirt,
and spinning above
are the many
silver batons.

Watch Your Head

Last Road Trip (alt.)

On our final pass through town
I am reminded of our agreement.

You said that if we ever break up,
you will smash this first clay-fired
cup we bought together.

Those were different times.

This is our last pass.
Our wedding china
now meets
the road.

Kevin Rabas

Answers

Look, I've had enough of this
waiting around
among the bookshelves
for you.

I know you're here somewhere,
like the ring the man leaves
in the poetry section, wishing
to make a woman his bride.

Watch Your Head

Phoenix

Let me rise up
like a wheat stalk:
my face hard,
my teeth many,
my whiskers long.

Out of me
make bread.

Kevin Rabas

Sunset

My friends, if I could call
you back, I would.
I would light the tiki torches,
set up the volleyball net.

But we are too old for all that.

We have moved on
and are married
and know our jobs
better than our loves.

We have joined
at church and at work.

We are no longer
for the simple joys.
A rose no longer strikes us,
and a sunrise is never enough.

Watch Your Head

Accidents

I will wait no longer
for our time to come.

I have heard your cry
in the night
and I am here
now to answer it.

Our lives together
begin with the sound
of light rain
on a wooden porch,
bricks breaking from
their sweat, cooling
in the dark of the city night.

Sirens are on the horizon,
and a chopper is overhead.

Everywhere
there are accidents
but here.

Kevin Rabas

Holding on So Long

You know how
men who sing the blues
never give specifics.
They just say
she done me wrong.
I am the opposite.

I tell you how we broke up,
what things she kept,
what things she left.
I let you know
what side I slept on,
how I still don't
stretch out.

She done me wrong,
I know it, but
I done her wrong
just as much.

And we both held
on too long.

Watch Your Head

Artt Frank's Jab

I took up the drums
as I had taken up
boxing, a welter-weight,
jab and jump,
turn and punch.
There is no time to rest
between bars,
only breathe.

I heard you
on the radio
on the way
to Korea,
and I prayed
that I would live
to meet you.

I not only met,
but became great friends
and performed with you, Chet,
most of the last
of your life.

We didn't play
bebop and cool. We were
bebop and cool.

Kevin Rabas

I never knew what you meant

I never knew what you meant
when you said, "I'm not in love
with you, but love you."

"We'll last as long as this china does."

"You see that mattress
on the floor. What do you think
it's for?"

Watch Your Head

[New Orleans, That Road Trip]

"Call me back when you're 30," she said. "And propose." And that's how we left it. That's how she left it. That's what I remember

We had been to New Orleans, and we fought all the way there and all the way back. While on Beale Street and in the hotel, we enjoyed ourselves. This is the magic of trips. They allow you for a few intoxicating moments to leave your troubles behind with the spare tire.

Full of gin and tonics, we spun and swung and danced in front of the man wearing the washboard; past the ladies displaying their legs on the stairways; above, a man on the balcony opened his coat and flashed the crowd below.

Kevin Rabas

Behind These Doors

Behind these doors
the words are opening up,
blossoming
with the abandon
of fall flowers,
which open only once,
the twirl of a skirt
before the freeze.

Behind these doors
I am writing you odes.

I am tasting
the honey
of memory,
then writing
like the good critic must.

Do not let these moments go
too quickly.
Dessert is still to come.

Watch Your Head

Apartment Warming

Allow me some time
here on your couch,
in your apartment,
and I will find a way
to shed new light
on your front room rug,
just a touch of amber
in winter's evening.

Know that I am
no simple man,
but a poet
with a knack
for lighting a room
with lamps and colored candles,
with words spoken low
over the glow
of fireplace embers.

Do not forget me
during the night.
I will be here,
waiting,
within sight,
somewhere
in the light.

Kevin Rabas

Grazie

You wake me
at 3 a.m.
to punch my ticket
and teach me the word
for thank you in Italian:
Grazie—
on the train
on the way
to Sicily.

"Remember," you say.
"Begin low like this
from the bottom of your chest,
then rise: *Grazie,*
holding the ah—
as long as you
can stand it."

We are no longer
in Deutschland,
you remind me.
Danka will not work here.

Watch Your Head

Make an End to Mourning

There is little room
for the black bird
of mourning
on your way to work
or during the lunch hour.

There is even less
for his shadow, grief,
while stacking and sorting
your laundry.

Nab him with a white cat,
which bounds from his
resting place
on top a red-tiled roof.

Eat these feelings.
There is little
time to grieve
while in the street
piñatas are being hung.

Kevin Rabas

Anna Karenina

Come on over
to the side of laughter,
Anna Karenina.
Weep no longer.

Let the men on horses
ride over ditches
and jumps
and break the backs
of their mounts.

This has little
to do
with you.

Leaven your bread,
and remember the man
who may rise
above the wheat.

Curl your hair
and forget
your many suitors.

There will be time
enough
when you
are ready.

Watch Your Head

Spring in the City

I have known the subtle
scent of spring
in the city.

I have watched the
water wick from brick,
and kids fill
the sidewalks,
the fountains.

Men sell flowers
in doorways.

Kevin Rabas

Spring and Fall

I have walked
through rose gardens,
reaching for a whiff
of petals
above thorns when spring
comes to the city.

I have followed
the paths of the student,
from one brick-booked building
to the next, sometimes forgetting
to eat, others to sleep.

I have watched the traffic flow,
first the white lights,
then the red,
over the hills.

I have wandered into the park
and sat silent as a sculpture,
waiting for the leaves to fall.

Watch Your Head

Swim Team Tryouts

I have known the sound
of my hands moving
like blades through water,
a string of bubbles
surfacing from the corner
of my mouth.

A kickboard slapped
on top of water
reminds me.
A tunnel of my peers
makes waves
for me to swim through,
an audition.

Those who swim
with strength enough
to overcome the kickboards
will become
part of the team.

Forget the solid safety
of dry land
and puddled concrete.

The water is
your only obstacle,
and speed
is not
on your side.

Kevin Rabas

I have known...

I have known a sadness, like ice, like sleet

I have known the unexplainable chill of
  indifference

I have known the mojito mixture of regret and
  grief

I have known the feeling of being crumbled into
  a tight bundle and left beside the edge of the
  road

I have known the end of something

I have known the joy of golden cymbals clashing in
  the sun

I have known the sound of hail on a tin roof

I have known the sound of tears splashing in a cup

I have known the sound of your voice
  in every mood

I have known the subtle scent of spring in the city

I have known where to put my hands

I have known the sound of my hands moving like
  blades through water

I have known the string of bubbles
    surfacing from the corner of my mouth

Watch Your Head

I have known the sound of crisp autumn leaves
    folding under tires

I have known the sound of june bugs ramming
    against the screen

I have known the glories of your eyes shining in a
    dark room

in homage to Theodore Roethke

Kevin Rabas

[Our Time]

Now is our time
alone on your sofa
facing the city
on your porch
on the third story
above the park joggers,
the winter lovers
hand in hand,
the singles walking
their big dogs,
the old ladies
with their handbags
and kerchiefs
to keep out the cold.

Watch Your Head

[Pomegranate]

The many-
hearted pomegranate,
fruit of the gods—
the dark red stains it makes,
and the sweet ichor
held in each heart—
goes on sale
one for a dollar
at the supermarket,

so we toss one
in our cart
and haul it
home with us.

Kevin Rabas

Chet's Unlikely Second Rise

> *"I don't play bebop. I am bebop."*
> *--Artt Frank, Chet Baker's drummer*

He came to our house,
his front teeth knocked out,
his spirit sunken,
his horn wrapped
in a blue towel.

Chet knew
he had to make
a comeback
soon.

I believed in him,
asked him to play
what he could.
His bridge slipping,
he played "I Love You,"
then scatted when he couldn't
blow.

He made it through.
His wife knew
he had to make it.
He had
three kids.

I took up the drums
as I had taken up
boxing, a welter-weight.

Watch Your Head

Jab and jump,
turn and punch.
There is no time to rest
between the bars,
only breathe.

Kevin Rabas

Waiting

I have known evenings
when the click
of the electric clock
is the loudest sound.

Watch Your Head

[for Doug Talley, on sax]

Playing sax so softly
you can hear his
keys click,
Talley serenades
the dinner crowd
at Elbow Room.
He breathes,
and you can almost see
the waves of heat
come from
the bell of his horn.
Tomorrow he will be
at some other bar,
moving through
faster, louder
changes. But tonight
his voice is soft,
whispering you
a few daily blues.

Kevin Rabas

Jazz Body Language

One nods his head
to the beat.
Another opens his mouth
just a touch,
as if tasting
each note.
One pats his foot.
Another bends
his knees,
sways.

Watch Your Head

[Radio Voice]

You play
the theme song
of the recently departed
jazz historian,
Dick Wright,
and I am reminded
of how his voice warbled
on the radio, mouth close
to the mic.

Kevin Rabas

[Merry Christmas, Kevin]

I have lost you
in traffic,
during the Christmas rush.
Your voice floats
to me. "Merry Christmas,
Kevin," you say, head poked
from a truck window,
my lost love, ex-wife.
Where did I lose you?
And how?

Watch Your Head

Voice

I find my voice
again hidden
small under the couch
in your apartment,
and I scare it out
into the open,
ask it to speak
louder, larger, rise
like a siren
and rush across the city,
flashing red lights and white steel:
Make way! Make way!
I can shout.
I can call you
home again.

Kevin Rabas

[Moving in]

This evening
again I consider
packing my bass drum
and moving to your couch,
so I can spend
every evening
with you.

Watch Your Head

Fall Golf

My sister picks wild pears
along the edges of the course,
while we play golf,
says she won't caddie,
even for her boyfriend.

And on the seventh hole
I swing, hit a walnut
right into the hole,
as a joke, wishing I had
simply pitched my own ball
that straight and true
from out of the gully
beside the creek.

Near the end,
I slice one
into an apartment complex,
waking someone,
I am sure, early,
while the dew is still
on the grass,
the birds clustered tightly
in the trees.

Kevin Rabas

[We took this town]

We took this town
in our late teens
one afternoon
with a bottle of Jack Daniels
between us.

We shouted at every poet,
turned our backs on every painting,
and plugged our ears to an entire symphony.
We were so full of coffee and spit.

Watch Your Head

Lend Me Your Lips

Lend me your lips,
my love, a taste.

I will hold you
until we share
the self-same heat.

Allow me a moment
with the small center of you,
and I will
reveal mine,
soft and full
as a muted trumpet,
a warm ray of brass.

Kevin Rabas

Buried out Back

They're no relative of ours,
but they're buried out back.   —Bertha (Keller)
                                        Rabas

The bones
are stored
under a stone
mortar and pestle
on top the hill:

a scout, on duty
even in the afterlife.
He tracks the sun,
first-light on the flat
horizon line
here in the land of fields:
Kansas.

Hunting pheasant,
my father and I
find a spent shotgun shell
and an arrowhead
together in a tire track
in an old
buffalo rut.

We hunt
the same lands
for the same birds.
Our weapons
the only difference.

Watch Your Head

We shoot.
One falls.

Tonight we will eat
our brother with wings.

Kevin Rabas

Because I Stayed

Those were the days
we would play
for popcorn.

We paid some dues,
rose slowly.

Many left
for New York,
Chicago, L.A.
Left for something
better. I stayed.
I am where I am
because I stayed.

Watch Your Head

Fool Self

I'll let my fool self out for you.
It's time you saw him, too.
Now is the time to do cartwheels
on the lawn, while the passengers
drive quietly by in their shells
of steel.

Wheel on! Wheel on
into tomorrow
same as today.

I know who I am
and what it is to play.

Kevin Rabas

Menninger's

I have known the cold sound the latch makes when
        it locks
behind you when the men in white put you to bed,
the paranoia of mirrors that house cameras
or viewing rooms on the other side.

You will know me even in my uneven sleep.
You will diagram my days and slate my meals.
You will hold me to my entire life,
    in one short group session, a graduate student
    jotting down what I have done on her yellow pad.

I have known nights alone in the city.
I have known nights alone at Yellowstone.
There is no sadness like this one,
    where I'm classified and typified
    like an ordinary laboratory rat.

At night you will give me one slim pill,
    which will carve a hole in my gut,
and there will be little left of me in the morning
    for you to examine and release.

Watch Your Head

Dreams

Beloved, know that in your blue room
I am spinning dreams for us both.

One morning, I will let you know my dreams,
like sand between our toes.

Let me rise from my soup
and kiss you full on the mouth.
Let us share our breakfasts
and know the crackle of a great
fire under the mantle
fed by wood we have chopped.

I am a dreamer, I know,
but I keep my dreams
so close to my hands
that sometimes there is no
distinguishing one
from the other.

Kevin Rabas

Not My Last Love Poem

This will not be
my last love poem.

On the highway,
changing lanes
in the dark,
I listen for your breath
on my neck, can
almost feel it.

Your scent
is in the front
seat with me.

Acknowledgements

The author gratefully acknowledges the editors of the publications in which these poems first appeared. Thank you.

"Knocking Out Walls with Chet Baker" in *Bear Review*.

"Together Now" reprinted from *Bird's Horn* [book] (Coal City Review Press, 2007) in a different version.

Words of Thanks

A big thanks to Curtis Becker–poet, writer, editor, teacher, good literary citizen, and top-notch individual. Thanks for editing and publishing this book.

Thanks go to Linzi Garcia for curating these poems–and for organizing them. Also, for typing them out. These poems have been "released from their cages" because of you, and they would have been gathering dust in three-ring binders in my office for decades without your love and care. You saved these poems. Because of you, others can now read them.

Thanks to Eric Sonnakolb for the great cover design work. Thanks to Dave Leiker for the photography work. You guys make things look great. (And sometimes you can judge a book by its cover.)

Thanks also to my parents, Joyce and Gary Rabas, for their enduring love and support. Thanks also to my mom for her copy editing help, although any lingering errors are mine. I unknowingly introduced them.

Thanks to Lisa and Eliot. Thanks to Alicia. Thanks to Dennis Etzel Jr, my poetic brother and constant friend and pen pal. Thanks to Joe DeLuca; it was a joy seeing a play and going out to hear jazz with you. Thanks to Kerry Moyer and Linzi Garcia for the blurbs. Thanks to Amy Sage Webb. Thanks to Mel Storm, Kevin Kienholz, Kat O'Meara, Max McCoy, and the EMLJ crew of colleagues. Thanks to Steve Catt. Thanks to Bob Dean, friend and pen pal. Thanks to Jason Ryberg, Jeanette Powers, Brandon Whitehead, and Will Leathem. Thanks to Tyler Sheldon. Thanks to Richard Warner. Thanks to Julie Mulvihill, Tracy Quillin, Murl Riedel, Valerie Mendoza, Leslie Daugharthy, Abigail Kaup, Leslie Von Holten, and the other good folks at Humanities Kansas. Thank you to Courtney Sleezer, Sagal Osman, Katie Donnelly, and Bridget Maloney. Thanks to Mike Graves.

Thanks to Ramiro and Irene for letting me use their basketball hoop for the cover photos.

Poet Laureate of Kansas (2017-2019) **Kevin Rabas** teaches at Emporia State University, where he leads the poetry and playwriting tracks and chairs the Department of English, Modern Languages, and Journalism. He has eleven other books, including *Lisa's Flying Electric Piano*, a Kansas Notable Book and Nelson Poetry Book Award winner. Rabas's plays have been produced across Kansas and in North Carolina and San Diego. His work has been nominated for the Pushcart Prize six times. The 2018 Emporia State Roe R. Cross Professor, he also is the recipient of the Emporia State President's and Liberal Arts & Sciences Awards for Research and Creativity. He is the winner of the Langston Hughes Award for Poetry, the Victor Contoski Poetry Award, the Jerome Johanning Playwriting Award, and the Salina New Voice Award.

Current Influences

MUSIC: Charlie "Bird" Parker (*Live at Storyville* and *Jazz at Massey Hall*), John Coltrane (*Both Directions at Once: The Lost Album* and *Giant Steps*), Keith Jarrett ("U Dance"), Madeleine Peyroux (*Half the Perfect World*), Miles Davis (*Kind of Blue*), and Lisa Moritz (*Dream of Blue* and *Holding Time*).

BOOKS ON TAPE: Laura Moriarty (*The Chaperone*), Bailey White (*Quite a Year for Plums*), and Michael Ondaatje (*Anil's Ghost*).

BOOKS: Tracy K. Smith (*Wade in the Water*), Mary Karr (*Tropic of Squalor*), Stephen Karam (*The Humans*), Kevin Young (*Brown* and *Blue Laws*), Aimee Nezhukumatathil (*Oceanic*), Traci Brimhall (*Rookery*), and Tasha Haas (*Certain Dawn, Inevitable Dawn* and *The Garden of Earthly Delights*).

Printed in the USA
CPSIA information can be obtained
at www.ICGtesting.com
LVHW040353061023
760079LV00015B/642